I Can Read!

SHARED
My
First
READING

Biscuit Flies a Kite

D0029061

story by ALYSSA SATIN CAPUCILLI
pictures by PAT SCHORIES

HARPER
An Imprint of HarperCollinsPublishers

Dear Parent:
Your child's love of reading starts here!

Every child learns to read in a different way and at his or her own speed. Some go back and forth between reading levels and read favorite books again and again. Others read through each level in order. You can help your young reader improve and become more confident by encouraging his or her own interests and abilities. From books your child reads with you to the first books he or she reads alone, there are I Can Read Books for every stage of reading:

SHARED READING
Basic language, word repetition, and whimsical illustrations, ideal for sharing with your emergent reader

BEGINNING READING
Short sentences, familiar words, and simple concepts for children eager to read on their own

READING WITH HELP
Engaging stories, longer sentences, and language play for developing readers

READING ALONE
Complex plots, challenging vocabulary, and high-interest topics for the independent reader

ADVANCED READING
Short paragraphs, chapters, and exciting themes for the perfect bridge to chapter books

I Can Read Books have introduced children to the joy of reading since 1957. Featuring award-winning authors and illustrators and a fabulous cast of beloved characters, I Can Read Books set the standard for beginning readers.

A lifetime of discovery begins with the magical words "I Can Read!"

*Visit www.icanread.com for information
on enriching your child's reading experience.*

For Liza, and for my many friends
at HarperCollins, who have kept us
flying high and free. . . .
—A.S.C.

I Can Read Book® is a trademark of HarperCollins Publishers.

ISBN 978-0-06-223700-2 (pbk.) – ISBN 978-0-06-223701-9 (trade bdg.)

The artist used traditional watercolor and Photoshop to create the digital illustrations for this book.

20   LSCC   13   ❖   First Edition

It's time to fly
our kites, Biscuit.
Woof, woof!

Look!

Puddles is coming, too.

Woof, woof!

Bow wow!

We have our kites. . . .

Woof, woof!

And lots of string!

Bow wow!

All we need now
is a bit of wind.
Ready?

Here comes the wind!

Woof, woof!

Bow wow!

Silly puppies!

It's not time to tug.

It's time to fly our kites.

Let's try again.

Ready?

Here comes the wind!

Run, Biscuit!

Woof!

Run, Puddles!

Bow wow!

Oh no.

The kites did not fly
high at all.

Let's try one more time.
Here comes the wind!

Woof, woof!
Bow wow!
Snap!

There go our kites!

What will we do now?

Woof!

Biscuit can run fast.

Bow wow!

Puddles can jump high.

Funny puppies!
You did it!

You got the kites!

Woof, woof!

Bow wow!

The wind is blowing.

The kites are flying high.

And you are the best
kite flyers ever!

Woof, woof!

Bow wow!